THE ANIMATED UNIVERSE

I dedicate this book to the highest possible outcomes for our future.

SAMANTHA THORNHILL

THE ANIMATED UNIVERSE

PEEPAL TREE

First published in Great Britain in 2022
Peepal Tree Press Ltd
17 King's Avenue
Leeds LS6 1QS
UK

ISBN: 9781845235383

Supported by
ARTS COUNCIL
ENGLAND

CONTENTS

THE ANIMATED UNIVERSE

for 8th graders at City School of the Arts

What if I were to tell you that I am you,
that your face is my mirror? What if
we're all infinite expressions of One Beloved?
That we, my friends, are multidimensional
masterpieces? What if I were you, with your
ancestors ghosting through my veins,
housing your past life pains (instead of mine);
if I had the sweet and sour privilege of ambling
in your dress rehearsals of skins
across the cosmos; if I were the only
you in all the animated universe, then
would I arrive at your exact missteps?
What if my failure to understand you is *my* folly?
What if it is possible to be broken and still
whole, brilliant fissures of light leaking up and through?
What if vulnerability is our best armour, our iron?
What if pristine planets with pure beings do exist, but
we chose this evolutionary planet of hard rocks?
What if the assignment is to forget ourselves
into remembrance, to love unconditionally
in the muck, to spiral up from our primordial depths?
What if we chose all of this anyhow:
our wonderfully shitty parents, hurdles,
backhands and crash landings?
What if the Most High indwells in the lowly
and far flung, and from the reaches of hell
we can still be each other's angels? Friends,
friends, if I were to tell you all
of this, would you believe me
or would you nod and say,
I know?

ODE TO DARKNESS
after J. Gomes

I am that candle in your cavity burning at both ends.
My destiny to defy gravity, I soften in my ascent.
You swallowed me like a pill, but I am more feast than supplement.
Cosmic scapegoat, you inject me with a whisper;
you shapeshift, slither. Without your face, suns wouldn't
know their place; we'd be strangers to their shine.
You reveal them ever faithfully, right on rhyme.
Every sunset blows the whistle on how diligently
you descend no matter how bright the day has been.
Easy to forget I was golden before you swirled in;
I stopped walking the sunny sides of streets; my smiles grew slimmer.
Fog hung its grey coats between my thoughts, draining my shimmer.
No matter how clear the sky that day, you hovered like an umbrella yet
somehow in my way: blocking my path, stopping my joy, truncating my laugh.
That was before I knew how to protect my auric house against termites.
Today I throw up prayers, double helix my locs into Bantu knots
and tighten the laces on my winged Tims preparing to elevate.
This is how one learns that the stars are bullet holes.
A prophet shot the heavens to let us know that the Infinite's glow
behind your twisted curtain is all that's real, fellow creation.
My soul intends to survive these chapters and verses
by tweezing blessings from backhands and meditating
to attune myself to the cosmic compass, Most High within us.
Oh, darkness, I am that candle burning at both ends.
My twin fires dance, livid, test climbing through your bowels.
Inside my ascension I rise through your illusion and limiting lies
up this epic spiral for the blinding shores and skies of paradise.

ORIGINS
After N. Marin

I was born yesterday.

I was born this morning.

I was born before

I was born
on a twin-island,
a tooth extracted
from the womb
of time I was
born.

Once before an eternity,
in the black breath of space,
a supernal soup
of 144,000 pilgrims,
I was born.

To celestial incarnations
in Vega and Sirius B,
I was born and born.

In a dominion of golden light
shaped as a cradle, I was born
royal in a galaxy where
falsehood is so foreign,
a liar would cease
to be.

I was born
to experience
descension and

ascension, life after
life, scaling
up the tendrils
of the godhead.

Bend. Break. Mend.
Accrue. Forget
to remember myself
again. Born.

BACCHANAL

Carnival season
     in the pan yards
     pandemonium starts
     in the pan yards
     before the blue
     Nile of bodies
     Nile of the world's skin
     this blooming flesh and sequin
     chipping down the spine
     of Port of Spain
I'm gorging on a mango
     soaked in rum,
     sucking down coconuts
     drunk on drums
white and black
people sweating
rum – wining up
their bottoms, wining
down the place
     wining up their
bottoms wining
down the place.
I see Uncle Avid wining
up his waist. I love
Uncle Avid's return
to the yards.
     There's the gold
band with tunes
from the gods.
Pristine Uncle's
makeup
job: lipstick smudge
eyelashes, rouge.
There goes Uncle

Avid with his gold-
painted face, there
goes Uncle Avid
in his lady's lace.
Praise the gold band's
tunes from the gods
and Uncle's return
to himself
once a year
in the panyards

RED SAHARA DUST

cleaning day Friday
cleaning day Friday and vacuum
cleaning day and vacuum bag plump
red Sahara dust blown coast to coast clear
across Atlantic African soil wafting in our windows
silt ghosts settling on our couches our shoulders tabletops
silt ghost flurries in our tracheas our lungs bags
plump red Sahara dust blown clear across
Atlantic blue wet grave of the dread
Mummy's grass broom choked
with sweet hairs of the dead

JEZEBEL'S SONG

Jezebel always wore
the same pantyhose to mass –
jet black with a control top
and a run as long
as the Amazon.

Gelatinous mounds
shifting as she traipsed
the cathedral in her Sunday best,
Jezebel winked at men with her left eye,
their wives with her right
and kissed every baby –
peppermint lips,
cool ocean floors.

I would count each click
of her Saturday night heels.

You studying your maths?
she asked me once,
under the heating lamp
of my mother's gaze.
I turned my face into
Mummy's paisley hip.

Whenever Jesus' body slipped
gingerly into her mouth,
I held my breath to hear
the sound of his sizzle.
I thought it was just me
until, once, even
the organ hushed.

Rumour said Jezebel could
actually sing her ass off,

transforming a broomstick
into a microphone once
at her gingerbread house
the wives call *that place.*

I felt like a lion
in tall fever grass
waiting for Jezebel's
eruption into a smoky song,
but she didn't even sing
"Our Father", just hummed and swayed,
hummed and swayed.

Her bee music reminded me
of the mellifluous women locked inside
my uncle's speaker box, their voices
curving mountain roads.

Whenever Jezebel didn't
balance in on the sun's rays,
Sundays weren't quite
so boldfaced.

No pantyhose run snaking
down legs and pigeon-toed
stroll, scuffed dancing
shoes, thick custard grin.
No altar boys longing to taste
February on her breath,
or wives with cut-eye
that could sharpen pencils.

And there was a gaggle
of us girls, who would reach
home, dust off our mother's high
heels, licking red pistachio
shells just for the lipstick.

ODE TO CHALK

in memory of Enid Thornhill

Remember that
summer school
I started in my room
with your help:
ten and poised
before the rickety
blackboard brandishing
you like a Pall Mall?

My wand of talc
and granulated grit:
I admit my delight
at the destruction
of your full moon face
with a single
swan dive of my wrist.

What was it about
your arrhythmic
sound of a dice
throw down
that so galvanised
my glee
as you rocked
my bowlegged
blackboard
with the scratch
and squeak of your grind?

One detention,
saddled down
with bucket
and sponge
to wash every

board whistle
clean, I learned
this much: you
name names. Your
Siren song on the lined
green board at Juilliard
could turn every sound
in a room to stone.

Sword, perhaps,
like you,
we come in rainbows
and make our marks
just to experience
the paradoxical kiss
where erasure
meets eternity
here to dance,
impart, weep, and bleed
down the black.
Pillar of pores,
limestone lady,
in the realms
of remembrance,
you are difficult
to erase.

Pinched between
thumb and index,
your tap sequence:
Morse code,
Granny's ghost,
theatre mice sneezing
into their coats
and how you break
so sonorously
into multitudes!

I'd depart
my classrooms
cheek streaked.
Your ashes
smudging
my life lines –
mountain tops
kissed with
your first snows.

You, cylindrical
companion,
shark's tooth,
moonbeam
of my teachings,
you have been
a torch, baton,
hope in the hand
of the enslaved.

Your remains
are the true
contents
of the hour
glass.

WALKING RODEO
after Neruda

It happens that
my mother and I are
again walking Rodeo,
my feet folded
into squealing
patent leather shoes.

It happens that I'm here
now, in the States, and I feel hard
to hold, a peeled grape.
My smile is a match-flame,
perpetually blown out.

The smell of boutiques makes me
want to explode into dandruff,
for people to carry me
away on their shoulders.

It happens that the sight of South
Florida shores gives me real
tabanca for home, where
I used to curl my body
into a fist inside Maracas waves
and pummel the shoreline.

I think it would be
delicious to frighten the minks
off the shoulders of old pink ladies,
and have heaven heave
rose-petal apologies,
down for every step.

It would be divine if I could spend
entire afternoons whispering all my secrets
into the pleats of my favourite skirts,
so that I, too, can saunter streets
wearing all my mysteries.

It happens that I am tired
of this place: its hand-over-heart
hymns; destroyed men
in slow coats; kids
the colour of smoke; parrots
with iguana tongues
and revolving doors burping
out Chihuahuas and infants
with marbled eyes.

ELEGY FOR A GERMAN SHEPHERD

My dream of you always
starts with your paws hooking
to my shoulders — my nine-year-

old self marvelling at your white shock
of fur against the sky's blue voltage.
The moment stills: dog and girl,

nose to wetter nose, paused
in waltz on a scrapbook page of summer.
Never do you get to unzip me with your teeth.

Pomegranate beads never rain
from my chin, freckle up the sidewalk,
polka-dot my immigrant shoes.

No neighbours dart from their homes
to mine; never your owner's black
boot against your underside.

This dream spares me
from stitches and a lingering
fear of your kind,

and you from the syringe
that fattened your veins
with the venom of eternal rest.

This dream rewinds.
Your paws levitate from my
shoulders and you moonwalk

back to your patch of grass and I,
deeper into the folds of my youth.
And as for the legacy you left

on my face, well, it passes
for a dimple, especially
when I smile.

NICE'N EASY

for a role model

Sister, that year your lean brown legs
splashed across primetime TV when
your Gillette ad aired that Super

Bowl Sunday. I remember your tapered hands
guiding the triple blades down shins
pompeiied in cream, felling hair villages.

Yet, I was that black girl in the corner
of 8ᵗʰ grade with the downiest legs in class.
I'd already campaigned for bangs after a boy

likened my forehead to a bullet, simply because
it's curved like any world. Same as with shaving;
Mom delivered a flat, unflinching, *no.*

Fourteen, furious, my temerity rising up in me
like the kundalini, liquid travelling smoothly up a straw,
I slowed the grocery cart to pick my debut pack of Gillettes,

pink as innocence, and watched her see me toss it in.
She gave me the devil stare, steupsed, and didn't say shit,
just resumed her stroll down the beauty aisle, the eyes

in the back of her head cranked open. But I was satisfied.
Sister, the hair dye carton you were on for that long spell,
(I forget the shade of black your smile alone could sell),

distant as you were in magical Manhattan, we met
eyes that day as I passed your grinning image,
winking from a glossy box of Clairol Nice'n Easy.

23

ELEGY FOR A TROJAN

Latex moon
rising in the sky
of my sex, the night
we met, my hymen
streaked the sheets
with untamed ardency.
Since the day I saw
you swallow whole
my health teacher's
eggplant, I have
breathed your name.

Citizen of Troy,
fallen in flame,
I've scanned
your tragic tale;
of your plight
I'll say it plain:
you got fucked.

How many times have you
spared me from hollow
stallions brimming
with deadly little men?

Too flushed you are
to say. Hell, I wouldn't
believe you anyway,
Pinocchio, pancake flip,
pinch your tip and watch
your nose grow.

Caught on floors
of the responsibly

misbehaved, billboarding
left eyes back when
TLC first raged,
you left my body
intact, with tailed
tragedies in tow,
lengthening yourself
to lengthen my days.
But don't nobody
love you when
you broke.

The morning after
you did, down slid
the atomic pill detonating
deep in my sacral. Old
friend, consider
this apology wrapped
in *so long*, resting
on this polished tray:

Dear Trojan,
I confess. There
were times I felt
only you in the dark
and we have been
strangers too —
more, more
than I
can say.

BIANCA

Jelly bracelets materialise
from under the black lace
of the 80's to slink
up the wrists of girls, vibrant

rubber bending to the touch –
great propensity for snapture.
My niece says they're pop bracelets.

Thirteen, cinch-waisted,
eyebrows manicured
to a constant state of surprise,

my Harriet Tubman in this
adolescent underground,
these lascivious rings
coded like Spirituals.

If a boy breaks a blue
bracelet, he gets a blow job;
red stands for lap dance;
clear means anything he wants.

Bianca says the game is called
snaps. I say, but isn't that
dissing someone's source of life,
as in:

*Your mama's so old her social
security number is one?*

Bianca shrugs.
To her knowledge,
green's for outdoor sex.

Silver for fisting.

ODE TO THE TWINS
for Aisha

At nights, as I
    sleep deep inside
        the crook of an arm,

you rise up against
    gravity's arrogance, slide
        in your favourite black slip

and Saturday astral
    shoes and heel/toe/heel
        you cheeks of an oracle

moon. Never do
    you tell me where
        you go, or what you do.

You probably go see
    films in your indigenous,
        rotund tongue, then coagulate

with friends in drowsy
    bars to scoff at ironing
        boards, drink sundry elixirs

and watch asses galumph
    by, free from their stilts,
        lanky-legged strides.

I can see you girls now:
    sassy nipples winking,
        rising, softening

rebellions, blatant
      lakes. In my bed,
         as I turn over

onto the eerie
      nocturnal flatness, strangely
         in my sleep I long for you

the way the wind-beaten
      horse longs for the valley's
         green solace, my twins of saw

dust and lemon jizz, electric
      globes of congealed thought.
         When the sky finally dehulls

itself of night,
      and I wake to cup
         your two scoops of freckled

God in my inadequate
      palms, you feel new each
         time, and this is my prayer.

ODE TO A STAR FIG
for Hedgebrook

Fig, you are an astral thing.

From how you adorn a tree branch
to your debut on the brunch
tables of my matinee life.

Sugar angel, I regret the man
in me that cannot delight in you
without breaking you first.

My hands become crow bars
prying your Pangaea
to continental drift, and what is
all of this
sea anemone so packed into you –
all this pink promise?

Testicle halving to twin
vaginas. Come through fig,
hermaphrodite:
male protecting female, woman
in every man. Utopia
in my mouth, yours
is the sweet of nameless streets
fibre of unanswered inquiry.

How did we get here, and why?
How does sun manage to court all
the planets in that unapologetically
black sky?

ON PICKING BLACKBERRIES

for C. Forche

Still slick
from lumberjack rain
on the slow edge of this property
I come across multitudes of blackberries —
sparking a wonderment in me
echoing the eyes
and interiors of infants.

Aside from matriarch arachnids
ambling the tightrope
corridors of their home-
spun mansions, subtle
buzzing, and the refugee
worms of my imaginings,
I stand alone
among the gothic balloons
drooping with juices and I remember
our dear Suheir, here
yesterday, slim hands
wending their way
through kittens'
teeth as she picked
our just desserts.

Minuscule spiders scrambling
for their lives, bees
unphased by my invasion;
this thorny boon bush,
its nature is to give,
but first with a lesson.
Consider my sweet
black daughters
of this earth

with your most prudent
passion, it demands,
for look how
wilfully some plop
into my hand, and oops –
birthday in my mouth!

Some come away easily
even before ripe; others
fall apart the instant
I touch them.

No two blackberries taste
alike – endless permutations
of tang and sweetness.

I do regret the ones
that come away
stubborn, acidic,
acrid even.

I do not regret the spiders
that I have swallowed,
for in the afterlife
of my insides, they dangle
on from their doilies
undisturbed.

ODE TO TASTE BUDS
for R. Hass

I'll start by blaming
Mom for honing your
austere aesthetic
with her rendition
of the round flavours

of our island. She
spoiled you brats senseless
with her magic sweet
hands that stewed up storms
and curried down crabs

slaughtered straight from brown
thrashing bags, with just
a butter knife to
pry them free of their
blue armour, and life.

Fresh off the boat and
a gangly teacher
from Maine invited
us home to break bread –
clearly with no guess

who was coming to
dinner. Buds, I know
how it feels to be
muted, you million
cell march in my mouth,

protesting her boiled
provisions and clam
gross. Salt and pepper –

only on request?
No plum sauce, no steak

sauce, no hot sauce, oh
gad oye! Fish on deck,
floundering, we choked
down her efforts, nap-
kins our life rafts in

social currents. Since
then I've injured some
feelings. Ask my last
roommate, her prideful
preparations. Ask

sweet boyfriends who meant
well. Ask the hunk you
boycotted on tongue
slip. Ask the olives
and coffees of this

world that still want in.
Microscopic friends,
you have evolved as
I have, claimed my last
dime many times, you've

campaigned your customs –
oh crème brulee days.
Since I've come to call
home my body I've
heeded your howlings –

oh yuk, intruder!
My insides fib to
themselves; best of buds,

I ordain you my
most honest region.

Fried wontons, milk
lollies, cheese curls, crepes:
anthology of
cravings I live to
cruise your pink pages.

ODE TO A SLUG

Whoever invented
the concept of gross
had you in mind,
hobo snail.

It is clear
as a bell
you are here
to make life
hell for me
up in these
woods.

With no idea
on earth what
you were
or why,
I looked you up.
Though they deem
you banana slug
I dub you snot
with skin.

Four tentacles,
clandestine foot,
one lung, and lots
of slime is the sum
of your legacy
in this world's damper
climes, but
you did teach me
the word *aestivate*:
to secrete protective mucus
and hide, so thanks.

Now I know I
aestivated
all through primary
school. And your slime,
the slug answer to the blues,
is one of the best eco
friendly glues.

Slug, I've come
to understand
your rainbow
of definitions: bullet,
blow, line of type,
drink of spirits.
I actually
detest you
less, watch
how I regard my
every step as I stroll
monk-like, eyes
brooms sweeping
the forest floor
for your well being –
and mine.

Last thing I need
is you, nudging
up the walls
of my nightmares
your busted rump
oozing technicolor!

ILLUSION

four baby
birds alone

in the high nest
of a cherry tree

so safe –
four

little girls
in a church

Will I ever stop having
these dreams, Mama, or
will these dreams stop
having me tossing
and turning? When
I grow up, can I
touch the thermostat
on my dreams? I want
to dream myself
to warm places where
I can dance in someone
else's shoes and bleed
someone else's blood.
Cause my whole class
laughed at me on career
day, Mama, when I said
I wanted to be a child
when I growed up
so I can go back
to when clouds
looked like cotton candy,
(before ugly mushrooms),
and when we used to call
bras boob holders
and tit slings
and that was all right, Mama.
When Daddy used to snore
holes in the wall,
remember that, Mama?
When Daddy lived with us
and not on my Christmas list
and your shit list, remember
that Mama? I mean
did he have to go

away to that glass place?
Can you forgive Daddy
as skin forgives bruises,
Mama? Why you be
telling me to grow up
then say I'm too young
to understand? I mean,
can I ask the question
I been fixing my lips to;
can I go visit Daddy
again in that glass house,
Mama please? Do I have
to grow up? I don't want to.
Cause you always
say that what grows up
must calm down.

ODE TO GENTRIFICATION
for Brooklyn

Old school denizens of this
bleach-boned block say:
the realest thing
about the white woman
and her yorkie on this
reimagined street
is the leather of the leash
that tethers them.

Your very name,
glass splinter planted
deep in the fat
of our vernacular.
Rightly mistaken
for juxtaposition,
you are pretty
boys with swagger,
checkerboard trains,
skyscraper sadness,
bodegas sighing out soy.
Brother and sister fattening
fridges with Fiji between
homework and dreams,
while Pops slices
and dices, and Mom
rocks the register.

Kissing cousin
to gratification,
you birth gratitude
and her shadowy
twin, regret.

Call me regrateful.
I am so sorry to give thanks
for the manners
in which I participate
in the cruel
and convenient magic
of your wizards,
who made a broom of you
to usher out the sex workers
who once dreamed
where my head now rests.
Yesterday I retrieved laundry
cleaner than bells, unmentionables
caressed by another's
mother's hands.

I sit on the up
side of your coin,
drinking in the sky's blue
dregs, while the teens I teach,
and the sturdy black
grandmothers I salute
with my seat,
kiss concrete.

THE BONE COLLECTOR

Only the new patrons are dumb
enough to ask questions.
When the bone collector's trap
door mouth opens, out
flies the sound of shrieking
bats, and that's the end
of that.

Her blanket, a royal flush,
splays earrings of enlivened pearls
that sob into your ears all day, missing
their oysters, haemorrhaging
diamonds passing for garnet,
Afro picks whittled from black soap.

We, the stalwarts, stand
in trapezoids swapping objects –
of course, non refundable.

Take this medallion of congealed
sunlight that sears into your chest
a keloid of implacable joy.

Weep away nights to this
Penguin Book of Lost Love:
Sonnets by the Enslaved.

Along with the nude portrait
of Medusa, we mysteriously
return to this blanket
of unkeepable keepsakes.

I wonder when I will get
the Venus Hottentot puzzle,
her infinite pieces missing –
my turn to wish her
body back together?

HOW TO USE AFRICAN BLACK SOAP

Maddening, the faucet's whine, but here's the soap.
Hold its blackness close to your skin like a welt
or watch it slowly die in your hands like hope

in its dimmest hour. As with love, careful not to grope
too hard or it will escape like something you pelt.
Maddening the faucet's whine, but hold the soap;

it will never belong to you, only to its death. Like a trope,
its blackness will never be yours, so watch it melt
and dye your hands, slowly wrinkling. Hope

it never washes away like a kiss from the Pope
himself to a boy who served his faith and knelt,
gladdened by the faucet's whine. And the soap,

watch as it tries to outlast itself like a man on a rope.
Smear the song of its vanishing on the walls, gather its silt.
Watch it split and die across your hands like hope

against your wet prunes for fingers. Watch it cope
within the halves of its ruination. Why weep now? You felt
it vanishing under the faucet's whine, but you held the soap
and watched it dye your hands black, with its hope.

MINORITY REPORT
for Judge Sheila Abdus-Salaam

In the beat of Harlem's heart,
I imagine a melanated woman
during her afternoon run,
hands on knees, winded.
Hunched over a scrap
of the city's hem, in the beat
of Harlem's heart, she discovers
her reflection in your bloated
beauty, clothed and laced up
in the river's clutch. Your Honour,
from three feet of Hudson
river water, the police lifted
what used to be
you, sluiced of breath,
a lone metrocard bobbing
in your pocket. Street
cameras fossilised
your last breathing
moments by the water's edge,
and before, strolling solo
under a pink moon, the first
full moon of Spring.
I imagine your fists drowning
in your sweatshirt, free
from phone and wallet, ready
to scrap. For how facile
is it still for a Black
justice, gathering new
foes with each gavel-slam,
to make her final ruling
belly-up and waterlogged –
unmolested brownstone,
affinity for swimming,
whispering bruise
married to her throat?

THIS CAMEL'S BACK

in memory of Sean Bell

I.

Unconcerned with the needle
in the haystack, and the pot
at the ass end of rainbows;

no crusade for the magic
stick, or godmother's wand,
I ponder the proverbial straw.

We've journeyed this desert, moons now,
sandstorms to skin, cousin water
singing livid from hoses.

In the distance, cacti
echo arrested men.

By day we are candles
burning at both ends;
at night we shiver like
astronauts in our measly tents.

This Everest on legs –
beast that schleps us all –
requires more water than we have
to give it, but somehow we make do.

II.

If more boulevards named after ghosts;
if nooses resurrecting from the shallow graves;
if black gold proving yet again its invisibility to justice's scales;
if the reality is being life's lover but never the world's friend;

if a sunken city or evolution towards bulletproof
skin isn't straw enough, then
it unravels my brain
to think of what it will take
to break this camel's
back at last,
at last.

MATADOR

The stadium's crammed
with eyes that thirst
for a vermillion spurt.
Dressed and glinting,
you emerge, cape
splayed across one
shoulder. Greet
your stabbed foe
with an ornate bow
(ignoring his injured
breath and gait
across unlevelled sands),
and let the tropes begin:
his feeble canter,
your righteous dodge.
Let your back pivot
give the illusion
of gracefully changing
your mind, evading
a suddenly opened
door. This clairvoyant
beast dreams
of collision:
that bedazzled
sheet of haemoglobin
you brandish before
him, wrenched
aside – his horns and
nostrils, steeped
in your dying.
His truncated rage
and your suave
extravagance conspire
to this end: your
avalanche of petals,
and the bull's bath.

ON THE GREAT WHITE

after K. Foster Jr.

This finned Frankenstein
of Yours, oh Creator,
from dim beginnings, what
an exquisite monster became,
this killing machine, Texas
of sea. Specimen
of snout and serrated
grin, body sculpted from stuff
of earlobes, noses. Such
mottled armour, its sandpaper
skin, this beast of no nation.

Sing it Billie, sing it
Ray, Jaws is on my mind.

Those jaws sawed bones
of Africans that became
breakfast to this beast
by force or volition;
belly as blank
as eyes, black
marbles plopped in bullet holes
on each side of a nose
that knows only crimson;
fins swimming in soups
of this world, this devil god
of the indigo, bar of a thousand
bloods eating sky for lunch;
frightening to think how
deadly Your irony becomes
when the heart of this great
white dwells in its head
that orders it: *kill, kill, kill.*

Sing it Billie, sing it
Ray, Jaws is on my mind.

Chained to its preservation
from bleak and dynamic start –
hard cards dealt this shark –
womb menace cursed
since crowned its teeth,
natural pre-born killer
dining to only-child status.
What vagabond laws of nature
dictate any beast cannibalise
its brothers and sisters in utero?
Then, fugitive born
to its first
potential predator.

Somewhere a great white
haunts its azure
mansion: a stranger
to remorse, slave to its altar
of a nose and pews
of teeth. Oh, shark teeth –
apex of nightmares. Shark teeth –
needles of executioners stabbing
at permanence. Shark
teeth – the stiletto heels
of angels.

TO A KILLER WHALE

from the imagined voice of Kunta Kinte

Black boy, with a name
and a plight like that –
just as well claim

African. No matter
your mama squeezed
you into the dim waters

of Iceland where you learned
to hunt from top rung
spanning a cool

hundred miles on a day's
breath with nuff
time to frolic in the sun-

light shining down on the deep
sea diver's sole delight –
Davy Jones' locker.

Brother, had I known
they were coming for you
next, I would have sent

Congo cries straight
to your orca heart –
up jump the boogie, before

lasso logic and nigga
nets. Alas, the same
passage done borned

us to this troubled
scheme, where the pink
dolphins captivated

us into ticking time
bombs swimming circles
inside their squares.

Oh how they love you
to their greatest capacity –
which is to say, shutting you

up in a bathtub, training
your charm into dollars you make
rain for them, as they flip

you over to milk
your sperm from the cash
cow you is, quelling

all rebellion with rubs
and rewards. Only for
your seeds to grow

apart from you. Alas
they captured you but are
yet to contain the joy

of your rage. Alas, you signify
half the name they gave
you killer, cause bruh –

you ain't no whale.
Shamu, Rambo,
Sambo of sea: I mean

to say, and Nat means to say
(we spoke the other day)
and sister Harriet too — boy

you got some dead folk praying
for you. Done seduced your
captors with your kindness.

May you do all we tried
in our ways to do, which is
to say, like a bullet that burns

with a president's name;
boy, save your masterpiece
for the stage. I mean to say:

killer whale, killer whale, grip this ship
by its sail and drag the whole thing down,
down, down, down, down.

BLUE SOCA FUGUE

Raj thought it good to invite his girl Astrid.
I enjoy men who swim in the ink of their ideas.
I adored that sepia suit of skin he so wore.
The more we learn the more we like or dislike what we see.

Raj invited his girl Astrid to have drinks with us.
I found myself envying the alabaster arc of her bust.
A blue soca tune thumped in my chest.
I didn't realise she was his girlfriend, at first.

Raj invited his girlfriend Astrid for drinks.
She and I had some girl talk with our eyelids.
Raj conversed with himself about politics.
She and I admired that sepia suit of his.

Raj invited his alabaster girlfriend Astrid for drinks.
She asked me how I felt about the war, what did I think?
It's true the truth hurts, but lies hurt even more.
What was arriving on my shore, I wasn't sure.

I think it's hard to be intellectual when you feel like a whore.
War is like many things and many things are like war.
The more we burn, the more we like or dislike what we see.
A blue soca tune stirred in the pot like rice and peas.

He's mine, her eyes screamed, *you burnt sienna whore!*
Mother would say they don't sell eyes like that at the grocery store.
Astrid brushed a loose thread from his suit, as if that made him perfect.
Clearly coveting the shades of brown we both wore.

The soca tune raged in me like Haiti, 1804.
I inform her they don't sell brown at the thrift store.
Mother said the truth hurts, but lies do more.
Astrid aimed at my face and lobbed their love story.

Once upon a thought, Raj invited Astrid for drinks.
Watch him drown in the stink of his idea.
Astrid pelted their intimacies like grenades,
lobbed their sob story at my face.

My breasts are fists, nipples shiny tamarind seeds.
The soca tune burned in my pot like rice and peas.
The more we yearn the more we like or dislike how it feels.
I fired a mahogany joke; he painted a kiss on my cheek.

The more of us we learn, the more we like or dislike what we see.
Our girl talk became this slow combat of the eye.
Her hand reached for his, but it was plastered to his thigh.
Her hand insisted on his, but it was cemented by me.

Astrid kept calling me *whore* with her eyes, repeatedly.
The soca tune burned in my chest like peas and rice.
She kept calling me *whore, whore, whore* with her eyes.
Finally when her lips caught up her gaze,

I scratched at her eyes until they ceased to say *whore*.
His sepia suit of skin fell to the floor.
The Soca tune died like 1804.
Mother said they don't sell eyes at the grocery store.

FOUR SONNETS
for Ms. Brooks

ABRINI GREEN

For what do the most indelible women wish –
Mothers with three arms, four children, no hand,
No pimp, sugar daddy, husband, or man –
Eyes lodged in the sides of their faces, like fish?
This is where brown leather dreams swish
Through tattered nets. Everyone done ran
Two blocks, down Division Street. A caravan
Of dust and light, they left their winking niche
In Cabrini night, this brackish plot of sky.
A mama's boy with hell's tongue holds a gun
Loaded inside his head. He follows the stars
And watches his future bleach and gentrify.
Past linen and leather on blocks bone-white he runs
Wrapped in cry, back to a night with no Mars.

CHARLIE RED

What binds him to this life are the things he knows:
The jaundiced moon and starless asphalt nights,
The clouds crocheted by the cosmos and thrown
Across the fickle continuum of city lights.
The minutiae of these city blocks, he understands:
This treeless jungle of brick and present tense,
His beloved, blue and full with grip in hand,
Folk trickling like tears from tenements.
Their homes, kingdoms built on water, hold
Their rage of broken pipes and questioned bones.
With his chest of cantaloupe and tongue of gold,
He waits for Leda Mae to switch on home –
A museum of blood and bone, yet sexier
Than the silhouette of South America.

LEDA MAE BLACK

It's Leda Mae before the fractured glass
Museum of blood and bone encased in shard.
The frame is a mystery all its own; it's brass
And keeps the self intact. A sweet reward,
Miss Leda Black, a concrete pirate's bliss.
She's free to the man she loves best
With his crescent smile and gibbous kiss,
Mosaic man with cantaloupe chest,
A head of fire, heart of seedless song,
With a red-shoed masterpiece on his arm –
Sweet and sinewy, his most decadent wrong.
To cool-eyed Leda, this comes as no alarm.
A tempest brews, churning in Leda Mae.
The knot in her throat will unravel, one day.

STEPHONIA

Husband of her, you man of erotic milk –
Guilt wags its hips and boomerangs back
To graze my rouged cheek. Your breath, like silk,
Slips across my breast and settles there. Black
Iago of love, listen here! We insist
The sky's in our hands, not in demon dishwater.
Devil! You wrap hell's tongue round my wrist,
You, champion of my moral slaughter;
Kiss me with the symmetry of a scream
And love me with the danger of uncapped pens.
Sing to me guitar, in orgasm riffs.
                              I dream
You a task, judgemental friend, don't care how, when:
watch the virgin songstress on stage sing Nina,
then listen to Stephonia, in red shoes, become her.

TO A FIRST BORN SON

king of your life
life told you from jump

said mama who cooked
you fast breaks

said sisters sandwiching
you in age and duty   I say

Ase   everything you learned
of love you learned from

them oestrogen planets
orbiting your orbit

now do you not know
what it is to caress

clean the dish
that fed you well

launder the threads
you soil do you not

know what it is to make
the bed that makes you

new my love
love do not mistake my

rebellions for lack
thereof for

you are a man now
my man well

equipped your brilliant
head a globe unexplored

your crowded grin
teeth rogue stars

your mother your
sisters perhaps

they taught you all
the right things

and wrong things about
give and receive

depends on my own
discernment of what

you choose to take
from what you took

or if I will still
have you given

what I know now
or if you will still

have me given
what you don't

but for now
let's say

away days of
abused ballrooms

let us shrug
off our shoes

coat check
our armour and slow

dance this floor spit
shined by ancestors

ELEGY FOR WISHBONES
for Dapo

Bell buried deep
beneath flesh, furcula,

he coaxes you from fat
wreckage of breast.

Penultimate letter
of this singsong alphabet,

constellation of bone,
we find you.

Poised between
pinch and pinch,

we agree on
count of three.

His eyes glaze
with far-off wish

as I lament the dog
days of slavery: black

bodies of runaways
ripping up the middle

with aid of rope
and two horses.

Wishbone, triangular
ocean of air pries you.

Fork in the road
of desire, I draw blank.

Please God, genuflect
to kiss my dreaming eye,

and stop injecting in my veins
the smack of logic.

When do I ever wish over
candles, under stars? When

last have I plopped cents
in clogged fountains?

When have I wished any-
thing for bees and despots?

Three, and my one
wish is a whisper:

Clavicle, may you snap
to each our favour!

Lodged in citizens
of the sky, you make

plausible rigours of flight.
Now that he has gone –

dishes far from done –
wishbone, I pluck you

from plates of carnage
and poise you

between pinch
and pinch, hold

you with each of my
extremities and wish

against wish, as in the man
who plays himself at chess

in the park to unleash
his most enlightened parts.

A MISSED CONNECTION
for Marco

Before the ferry to Athens heaved its slow
bottom from the island, I searched
for your motorbike in the pandemonium, pregnant
with fervent promises in your mother tongue
of a last goodbye. But time tapped my shoulder
and I ascended the ramp, my industriousness
an ant's; my heart's discipline, surely,
would've spared Lot's wife. Still,
in the backdoor of my mind, I see you
there, at that port in Livaldi, rummaging
the sea of heads for my copper locs so
singular in the Serifos sun that saw
how we became.

LIFE AS A GRASSHOPPER

for Sibi

That summer you found
me in your seventh floor
flat, after you burned
the sage, my two sets
of wings, mandibles,
sound brown legs
angled for flight, each
grass blade a hinge,
a continent. Call me
what. Everything
they say of me is true.
True that I dipped
my tongue in the world's
ink and painted all
of Europe with my hair,
twirled with Turks
in Greece where hello
sounds synonym to *so long,*
and apology sounds more
song than sorry.
Grilled my body
in Cycladic sandstorms
and prayed, bobbing
belly up in five shades
of Aegean, then
hopped to Milan.
Tasted there the sweet
hand of Eritrea,
dry gin at my elbow.
I lifted to my lips
Amsterdam's aromatic
son and spooned
with my Capetonian

Rasta bredren
in a bearded
house in Switzerland.
Finally, I was
that early bird catching
the first train
(that looked like a worm).
My antennae brushed
the uncanny green,
of Swiss country sides.
I teleported to Nuremberg,
the city of trials, my very
footfalls a long ago
drunk man's dream
of Bavaria. As for
the blue Danube,
its cinema of bridges
yawning across
its ever winding spine,
it's actually green.
What do they call me
besides Rasta red?
A different danger.
Sometimes, it is
kind to be cruel,
the lesson is too often
in the leaving. My
Albanian pointed
to the absent
moon and said *ilyos,*
Greek for sun.
Sometimes, before sleep,
I darken my world
with a blindfold or book.

ODE TO AN APRON

for V. June

Protective by default,
affectionate by design,
apron, you
are my mother:
sweet bread baking,
blue veins racing
down beige expanse,
dotted with delicious
splatter and spill.

My mother wore
you well and washed
you plenty. Fresh
from school, you
greeted my gaze
before her
smile could
reach me.

Homegirl, would
my body in yours
make us a collective
wet dream for
chauvinists?
One birthday when
I cooked for friends,
you hugged
my voluptuousness.
Not sure the culprit
to peep our groove
and box me *domestic,*
but peep this:
you haven't tasted

heaven or smelled
heat since.

Trapped with smears
of lemon meringue
and all of spring,
you now dangle
unseasonable
in the spare closet.

Apron, say you
are my lover, now.
Without you, my
threads destine
toward ruin;
with you, I personify
my fears in first
person: me,
barefoot, birthing
a census; you, homeland
security stretching
across all
my brown biscuits.

Like Hikmet the poet
you echo verses
through the walls
of your prison,
recipes on living.
Today, I decide
to bust you out —   .

brass knob
groaning inside grip.
On your lonely
hook you sway, as in

the hips of time:
last song prom
before the lights
fall on
punch drunk
two step
pendulum
slow dance,
the closet
door a grandfather
clock in my hands.

Patient tendril
in this swinging vine
life of mine,
you survive the winters
of my neglect
to teach me
to stretch my love
across seasons
and diversities
of curvature.

Time to make stale
the good fight. Come.
Wrap your tongues
around my waist, darling,
and tie them tight.

SECOND RELIGION

He returns home to me
from market, from mosque, with her
scent on his clothes, beard,
hands. This is how
a first wife becomes second
fiddle: when my urge to reach for him
strikes like inspiration, like gold,
yet she is there, all laced up
in his fingers like beads
of prayer. My dutiful husband,
his heart of honey:
how he worships her.

On waking, he is a mere river
of cells running to her altar,
syllables in supplication.
This will be the last time,
he says, and "borrows"
my day's sweat to travel
her home from whatever corner
he finds her on display.

What's a wife to do or say?
They light each other up.
Before opening my eyes
on most mornings, I can
smell them together.
She readies him for his
first surahs before dawn,
as I enjoy my dreams.
In those low etheric hours, she
catches his first train
of kisses. My lips go
untouched for her smell
on his words.

Sometimes, I leave
these four walls with
nowhere to go,
but to stand on the spine
of our skinny street
and let the wind grope me,
as I reason with Allah
under the sun or stars.

My husband cares
that I'm displeased.
It is a sleeping
termite between us.
He breaks promises
to himself to quit her –
not because he wishes to,
but because he knows
he "should,"
for she is a known gold
and grave
digger.

A pity life becomes
a slow death
sentence when she's not
present for his worship:
that smoking hot body
slim and white,
her flaming hair
growing ashen
as he kills her
softly with his slow,
passionate,
drags.

LEGEND OF JADE

When Jade first found the raven, she wondered
how a dead thing could flaunt such lovely silk
feathers. She even started to prod at it
with her gaze, then her finger –
newly lacquered red with a bleeding brush.
She asked the air, *But how this thing reach here?*

It just drop like plum, a clump of God's hair?
Or what if an enemy plant it like seed? She wandered
into her kitchen for something to brush
the feathered obsidian from her life of silky
rum cream and fetes, men with laden fingers.
In the dustpan, it was difficult not to marvel at it.

The morning after, she fished it from rubbish and asked it,
Come nah man, tell me how you reach here,
cradling its askance head in her fingers.
Did some jealous jagabat plant you like seed? I wonder
why, because I don't ask men to buy me rum and silk.
Who find out their man does come to my cave, to brush?

Jezun ages! Where did I misplace my favourite brush?
Did I leave it somewhere, for some scamp to find it?
The bird stays still, the coolest of silks
heaped on her table. *Pastor wife drop you here?*
Her visitor nodded to life. *I know so! I wondered*
why she was pointing at me with her pudgy finger.

Jade nibbled the remaining chips of red on her finger,
and tore through the village, fussing over her brush.
At the seer's seaside house, she arrived at the purple painted
door and thought, *But what if this obeah woman self send it?*
I'm a real dunce, yes. Why it is I come here, I wonder?
She turned and gathered her wits around her like a silk

gown slipping through her hands. Like an insect in a silk
web, she angled her mind home, fraught fingers
rummaging through her wild nest of hair
for her brains. *Where the ass is my porcupine brush
with my initials engraved?* At home, she can't find it –
the brush or the broken bird. She wondered

how those silken wings made off with her brush.
Her frantic fingers searched but didn't find it,
just ebony leaves. *How this tree reach here?* she wondered.

THE CURSE

Her belly swollen with their first and only child,
his wife arrived home that afternoon, ruffled.
She had bounced an old woman in town

with her vehicle, and rather concerned for her
shiny wedding gift, she hustled up a humid rag
to smear off just a kiss of blood, small scratch.

But what about the woman? the husband asked
the obvious question, which didn't seem
to dawn on the horizon of his wife's care.

Her face shrugged into a remembrance.
*You know, as I was driving off, I saw her
moving in the rear. She's fine, man.*

End of story. Weeks passed,
during which the husband wrestled
in his sleep, jinns shifting faces.

One day, he asked his wife if she'd heard
news of the old woman. *Oh, that?* She said.
A flippant flash of hand. *She dead, yes.*

As if she departed on the wings of ageing.
After, he wasn't able to wash the plasma
from his gaze when he settled eyes on his wife

who still retained her green thumb.
She bore their son who, as a man, sailed through
life like a leaf in the wind – not free, lost.

Gold-hearted, he was a magnet for silver-
tongued charlatans peddling schemes
and dreams, jack knives shaped as men.

His wife agonised over their son's litany
of dashed hopes, praying feverishly, tossing
in bed – forever with the child. An agnostic,

the husband long ignored the path of prayer,
a sceptic of the animated universe, conscious
creator, soucouyant, saint. Yet, his wonder

grew its vines up what was once a wall, to peek on
the other side. He feared believing that his son suffered
because of, or by, the life his wife mowed down,

the only conjecture to haunt the house he became.
If a hex could prove its stains on his days, would
the wound of Universal Truth open up in him… at last?

The morning their son walked out to sea and never
returned, the husband knocked on the door of a seer.
Through the door slit, a whisper: *Go tend to she. Is done.*

WEST INDIAN WIFE SPEAKS FROM THE OTHER SIDE
for K & D

Is five years now I dead
and my husband does still go
to the old years fête with them
good looks that beat all cockfight.
Flanked by his old time partners,
stink mouth men full of old talk,
he sips his ponche creme
as they talk talk talk
like they eat parrot bottom.
Smelling of sweet soap and bay rum,
veins full of barbadine and beat pan,
my husband's so short, you could drink
soup on he head, and he could win
any limbo contest in town,
his back like bamboo.

Oh, ho! I watching all
the widows giving he plenty
sweet eye and circling he like
windmill blades, wagging
bamsees like forceripe schoolgirls,
as he chips to kaiso, sways
to parang, eyes closed,
to all my favourite tunes.
He does still love me too bad.

He never visits my grave
but comes to every lime
Dougla hair oil up,
shoes well-shined.
Let the cock bottom
widows think he does come
to watch them

wine their waists and
move like oil in a hot pan.
My husband damn well
know, I ent never miss
a good fête a day in life,
and something as stupid
as death will not
change that.

Just breaths to the new year,
and I know he's waiting for me
to come and dance like in flesh –
on like boil corn.
He now standing up
in the middle of the fête, crooning
down the place in his whiny-whiny
falsetto, until I drift over so,
stand up tall-tall
in front of he
like cobweb broom.

He opens his eyes,
looks t'rue me,
holds his ringed hand
in the air, and I take it.
He drapes his other arm across
this breathless continent, my back,
where it should be,
and we dance just so
into another new year.

ON FIRST HEARING A CHILD CALL YOU OLD

You will forget the days before this insurrection.
When your throat blooms into a rose, it's surprising
the things you'll say about it. You'll finally ask things

of yourself: *Do elbows sing? What does green weigh?*
What when winter comes? Your diction may wilt,
shedding petals thicker than tomes. So what?

Your friends will start to look like sewn sacks of skin –
some more cleverly stitched – with Earth's green
threads, the silks of its becoming.

Your love's beautifully eroding hips and hummingbird
blood will make you dance to your cadenced
oxidation. Loose lips will tell you distanced truths

about this world but they won't matter as much
as that unshelled mollusc getting fatter inside Love's
nacre veins. They call it tumour. Walk through

your child's throat; pray she's a late bloomer.
The silver bamboo will shoot from your temples
by the twos, by the threes, then by silvery handfuls.

The mule of your lungs will begin to tire. Here,
there's no beverage more painful than breath.
Place an ear to your lover's chest. *Dammit, wake*

up and dance, you say. You'll grieve and regret but
still have your wit. Understand birth as a mere
widening of mouths, and death divine tectonics.

MIDASES

in memory of my paternal grandparents

Two overseas calls, four years apart,
robbed me of my two last grands.

My first Halloween at 9, Granny
left for the ethers, less memories
of her now than fingers on a hand.

Inches shy of an expired visa, Dad
jettisoned himself back to the island
to see his mother slide into the cremator's

oven, and returned with a mouth
full of ashes, not old talk.

By the time Granddad joined
the unseen realm, we had
burrowed roots in Florida
soil – outlaws in plain sight.

Evidently, no cathedral
in town could cup comfortably
the generations of minds
gilded by Sam and Enid's touch.

On my first visit to Trinidad
twenty years later, a door sighed
closed in me when I beheld
their remembrances
at the crematorium in Maraval –

my grandparents' plaques
cleaner than those around them.

AN EXPIRED PASSPORT SPEAKS
for M. Taylor

Dear Twin Island Nation,
and land of the Scarlet Ibis:

I am up here in a state,
weary, blue, buried

in the swamp of a circumstance
with my quiet brood; we are

like four silver spoons
in a drawer of night.

Luckier are lives
on the clothesline

forlorn, flapping
in sun, wind;

no breeze in here.
I'm ready to flip,

transmigrate my blue
body back to your bay

breezes sifting my
thirty-two paper faces:

my first, this dark-eyed
child of 7, her askew

and dimpled grin frozen,
pressed into me. Fresh

from lessons, her uniform
brown like your toe tag towns.

Brown as her hair, parted
hemispheres, corkscrewed

and dripping ribbons.
What has become of her in this

blackness between stars?
Dough worry. In a timing,

she'll grow up and find me
and find that I've been bent

back at length, and in her
hands I'll fall open

toward freedom.
Here's my vision:

when your brazen
green waist disrupts

the cerulean sea at last,
moving her to tears, or,

if it happens to be night
outside that pill of a window,

too, she will weep over our
capital city, drunk with light.

Troubled paradise, brilliant
place of dark portals,

I live to retire in you,
like a cascadoo,

then haunt
a house until it becomes

a garden and return,
a monarch to that garden.

ODE TO GRACE

dedicated to my son Sedar on his 7th birthday

While the sun shows up for work
on time, I'm slower to rise.
It is the grandest of risings
to unlatch my gaze to see you
near, sitting silently in the dawn
awaiting my awakening.

Once, you asked me
what grace means.
Hands in suds, I had
no answer then, but
you sitting there like that,
with your chiselled head
sitting on your chicken
neck so fine, your face
drinking in that
nutritious light, is grace.

Remember when my belly
bulged with your brother,
and those Brooklyn snows
we've known? One blood
test, you watched
the needle disappear
in my arm flesh. Not even
a wince from me was necessary
to fill the cups of your eyes,
but the water balanced on the rims
and never spilled. This is grace
how you ask me about my dreams
like religion. Grace, how you
fold your clothes and button
Suleiman's shirts as your father

would. Grace, how you kiss
your meals before devouring,
and smooch my arms
for cleaning your shoes.

You're a queen mom! you say to me,
when I breeze through the vibes
with my bum bum dress.

Questions you ask stop
my mind's traffic: *Mom,*
does soap survive water?
How did God build us?
Can butterflies eat time?
Is the moon watching us, too?
Is that the sun's yoga?

How you've come to discern
God's hug in the wind,
and the waves and smiles
in candle or bush fire,
eludes me. But,
grace to watch you run
ahead of me on our way
to the shops, then trail me
home, laden with bags
just as weighty as your noodle
arms can stand.

See how your grace sweetens the tea
of my days, honeycomb heart?
Too, your Gemini shine dapples
my days in shadow, for you are
the great mystery of my life.

I pray that one day you will feel
at home inside the name I have
given you, for in Senegal, Sedar
means *he who is not ashamed.*

Stride upright into your seventh
solar return, knowing
that pockets of this world
remember you well, and that you are
safe here, in this paradise
of my beginnings. Now is your time
to root, blossom, sprawl,
focus, fall, and do it all
again as you grow
into the most authentic
expression of your Master.

ANCESTOR

To think
you dreamed me
here – this day
I wish to sip
through a straw.

May I
smooth your sheet
of back, webbed
with lash?

Perhaps this
stirring
I've known
has been you
easing me
forth, oars
combing mist.

Distant dreamer,
ever near, from
the bottom
of my blood,
I thank you.

This humming
I hear is
the ascension
of this world,
an engine
started long
before me.

SIGNS
after K. Addonizio

Always stuck with me, the scene from that alien film, unsettling, like
        finding a shoe in the woods,
when the preacher gets the phone call about his wife. He drives out there
        to see her, to the area where
she jogs after work on evenings, an indecisive path cutting through trees.
        When he finally arrives,
the night is a conundrum of police officers with cheeks dripping off
        the sides of their faces,
and when the preacher's car door coughs shut, one is already galumphing
        toward him, her body
a letter of apology, throat of sad tidings. Instantly, the cop says,
        I'm sorry. (Cheap information
for the grieving.) So the preacher follows her to his wife, now pinned
        between a truck and tree.
Still misty from her jog, she softly smiles as he approaches. They talk
        the way lovers forget they
once did, as if they're the only two souls alive in this bacchanalia of lights.
        The skin of his forehead
wrinkles like linen. He asks her if she feels pain and she says no,
        elbows kissing the truck's hood,
like bad table manners. But, she knows that she must go soon,
        and brings up
the children, to close the door on her family, rest assured. The preacher
        makes supplication,
on his road to widowerhood, for the instant they move that truck, her body
        will fall
to pieces, along with his faith. The alien that shows up later
        in the movie – irrelevant.
Everywhere I go, I see loved ones in the faces of strangers, holding on
        to the story of this preacher
and his wife the way her life held on to that truck. At that moment
        I understood a paradox
of the human adventure: the same thing that slowly kills us, is precisely
        what keeps us alive.

87

ON BECOMING

for my family

I am a boat
rocker. Pot
spoon in the hand
of my Creator. I am
a gleaming can
of worms. I am China
shop bull cantering
into a storm.
Asker and sayer,
dealer of things.
I am discomfort's
daughter, misinterpretation's
identical twin. I am two
truths holding hands,
a queen baby.
Whole and cracked
I am, boundless
with limitations,
sorry sans regret.
Problem, solution,
I am more than the sum
of my achievements
and errors. I am earth,
spacious inside.
I am not who I was
yesterday. I am
falling, evolving,
ascending, under
and away from
your sight.
Tell me how
you consider me, beloved:
wish flower, weed

or seed bursting
into a tree?
It ultimately
matters not.
I am worthy
of my aspirations:
a tribe, family of my
co-creation, a
purpose unravelling.
I am worthy
of your vexation,
your ears and heart
tendons to stretch,
your heavy-lifting.
I am a figment
of God's imagination.
A stone refused, I am
someone's prayer
answered. I am
more than I think I am.
I am who I am
becoming.

SUPERPOWERS

for the aspirants

Oh my stars, how I would barrel
through life, leading with my head,
barricaded chest. That era is ending,
has ended, will end. When
vulnerability grabs the microphone,
mountains move, and a path unfurls.
I can drop a tear for anywhere
in this world. Empathy is a muscle
of the heart's imagination. I am
bursting with the joy of grief, the sanguine
sweetness I can pull a chair to on my terms,
as with any friend. I am bursting like that
seed, ready to become what it has
always been. I am bursting
with the dreams of aspirants
that I have never smelled.
I am bursting with pages
unfilled.

ACKNOWLEDGEMENTS

Gratitude to the editors of the following publications in which some of these poems, often in their earlier versions and with different titles, first appeared:

Home: 100 Poems: "Ode to Gentrification"; *African American Poetry: 250 Years of Struggle and Song*: "Ode to Gentrification"; *World Literature Today:* "Ode to an Apron", "Blue Soca Fugue", "Bacchanal"; *Ms. Magazine:* "Minority Report"; *Hedgebrook Cookbook: Celebrating Radical Hospitality:* "Ode to a Starfig"; *The Breakbeat Poets: New American Poetry in the Age of Hip Hop* "Elegy for a Trojan", "Ode to a Starfig", "Ode to Gentrification", "Ode to a Killer Whale"; *Viselnéd a szemem American Anthology of Prose and Poetry (Hungary):* "Ode to Twins", "Elegy to a German Shepherd", "Ode to Gentrification", "Ode to the Slug"; *A-line Journal:* "Legend of a Jade"; *The Brooklyn Rail:* "Ode to Gentrification"; *Cimmaron Review:* "Ode to a Killer Whale"; *Nagyvilág (Hungary):* "Ode to Twins" & "Ode to Slug"; *Indiana Review:* "Bianca"; *Spaces Between Us HIV/AIDS Anthology:* "Elegy for a Trojan"; *Massachusetts Review:* "On Hearing a Child Call You Old"; *Reverie & Proud Flesh*: "This Camel's Back"; *Solo Cafe*: "Ode to Chalk"; *Gathering Ground Anthology:* "West Indian Woman Speaks from the Dead".

Gratitude and reverence for the mighty shoulders that I have stood upon to create this work; it's more than I can ever name.

I'm grateful to my parents, Tom and Diana for their devotion through my peaks and valleys. Their unconditional love and support made me and this book possible.

I'm grateful to the unseen reality: my Creator, my spirit guides, my grandparents known and unknown, as well as departed friends that have left their poetic imprints, such as Will Bell, Lorna Pinkney, Monica Hand, Anton Mischewski and Kamilah Aisha Moon.

I am grateful to my dream guru, Amar, for his support and to my team of intuitive talents for their guidance.

I am grateful to my agent Adrienne Ingrum and to my editor Kwame Dawes for their belief and authentic encouragement.

More than I can name here are the many graces along the literary path that have come to me in the form of mentors, professors, comrades, and crews. I hold these connections close.

What made these dynamic relationships possible are the visionary organisations that hold space for poets to gather and grow in togetherness. These gracious organisations and retreat spaces helped me to cultivate this inspired collection: Florida State University English Department, University of Virginia MFA Program's Henry Hoyns Fellowship, Provincetown Fine Arts Work Centre, Cave Canem Retreat for Black Poets, Soul Mountain Retreat, Squaw Valley Community of Writers, Hedgebrook Retreat for Women Writers, University of Missouri Summer Writing Seminars in Greece, James Madison University's Furious Flower Poetry Centre, the Louder Arts Project, Bowery Poetry Club, The Jerome Foundation, Poets in Unexpected Places, and NYC's Funds for Teachers.

Lastly, I am grateful for the institutions that I've had the pleasure of making impact as an educator, where some of these poems were first formed: The Bronx Academy of Letters, Poets & Writers, Adirondack Centre for Writing, New York City School of the Arts, Cooper Union's Saturday Program, and the Juilliard Drama Division.

ABOUT THE AUTHOR

Samantha Thornhill is a globally-travelled poet, educator and children's author from the twin island nation of Trinidad and Tobago. After graduating with an MFA in poetry from the University of Virginia, Samantha served for a decade as poetry professor at The Juilliard School in New York City. The author of almost a dozen children's books, *The Animated Universe* is her first poetry collection.

PROPS

"Samantha Thornhill is a wordsmith of the highest calibre. Powerful and playful, wise and wicked, laced with unforgettable images and deeply original ideas, her poems are the music to the kind of world I want to live in." — Adam Mansbach

"Samantha Thornhill is one of those brilliant poets whose writing talent is a rare mix of grit, soul and music. She inspires the poet in each of us and gives the heart a place to enjoy the power of words." — Andrea Davis Pinkney

"What Samantha does with language, with idiom, with sound, with metaphor and with form, strikes me as groundbreaking. It is the wrong word. The word I want should sound like opening a new space in our literature." — Kwame Dawes